ABC
Coloring Book

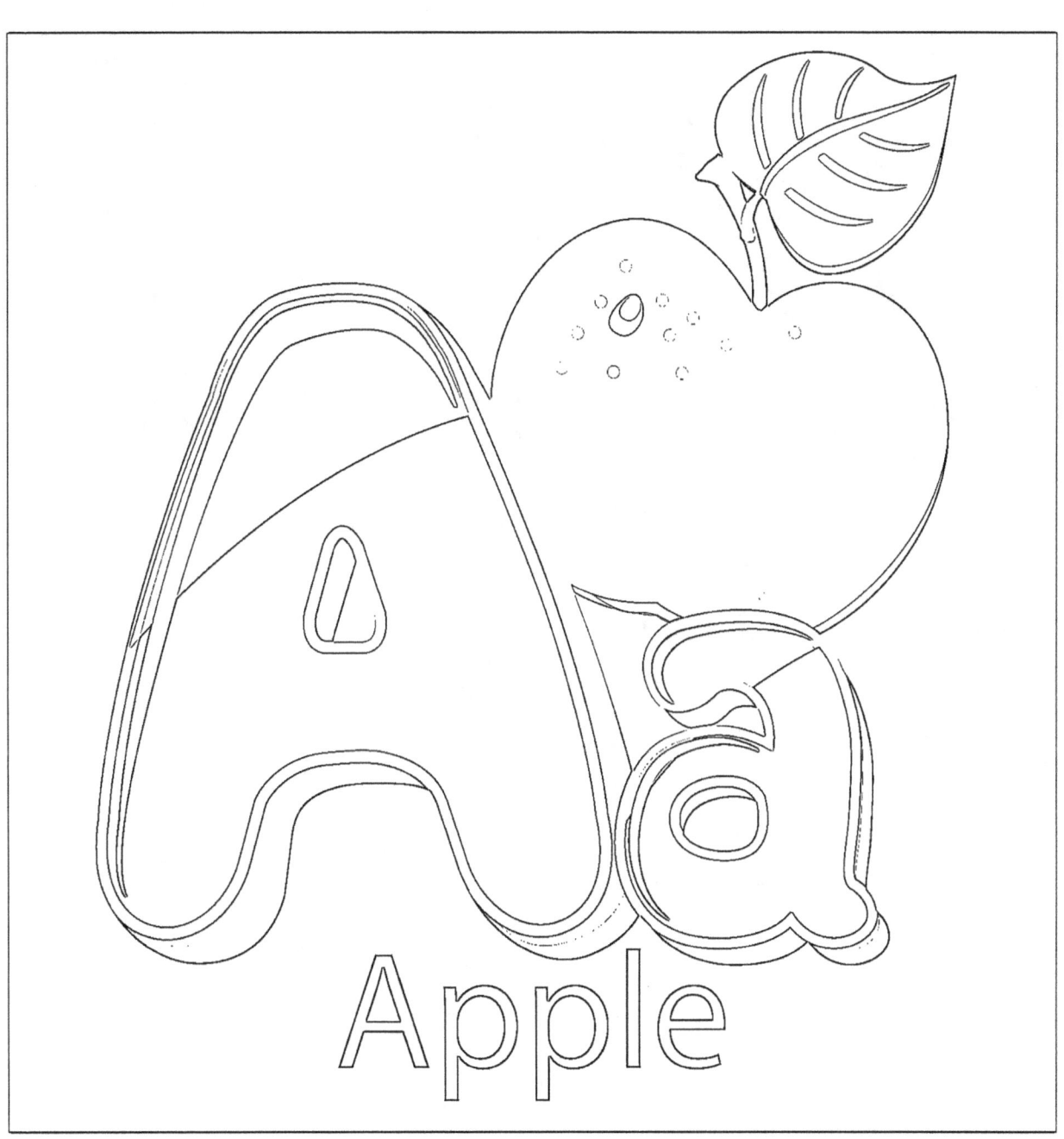

Apple

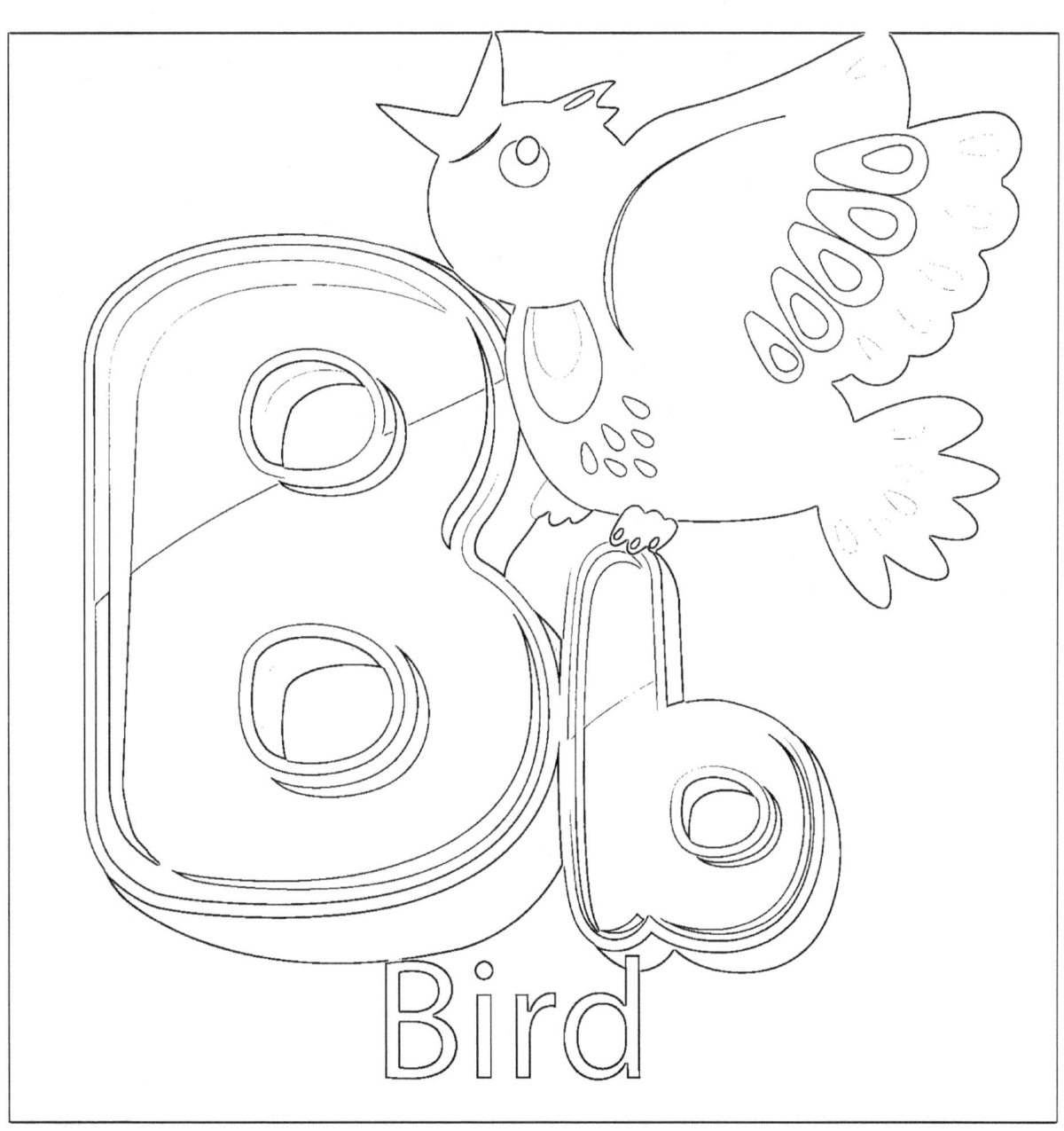

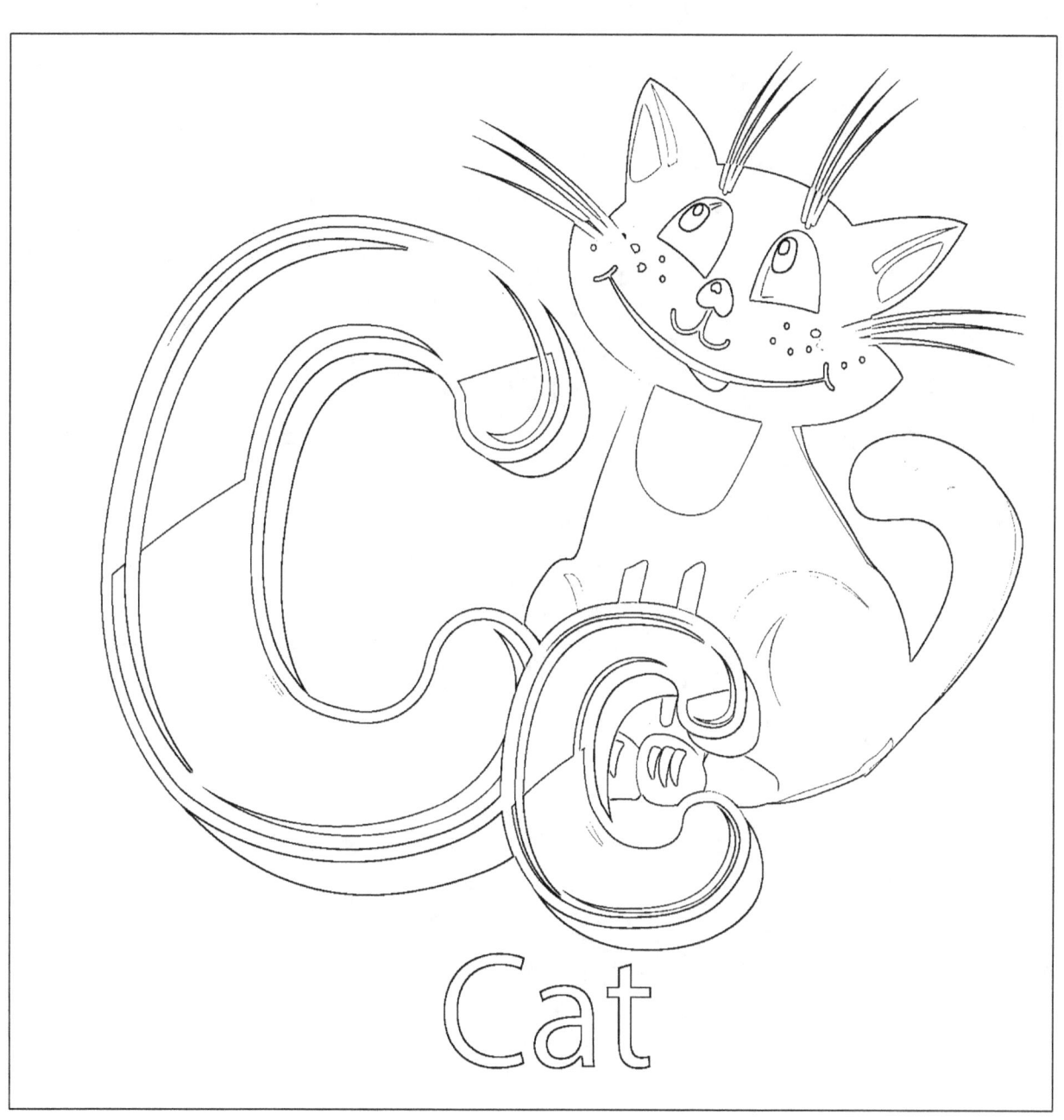

Cat

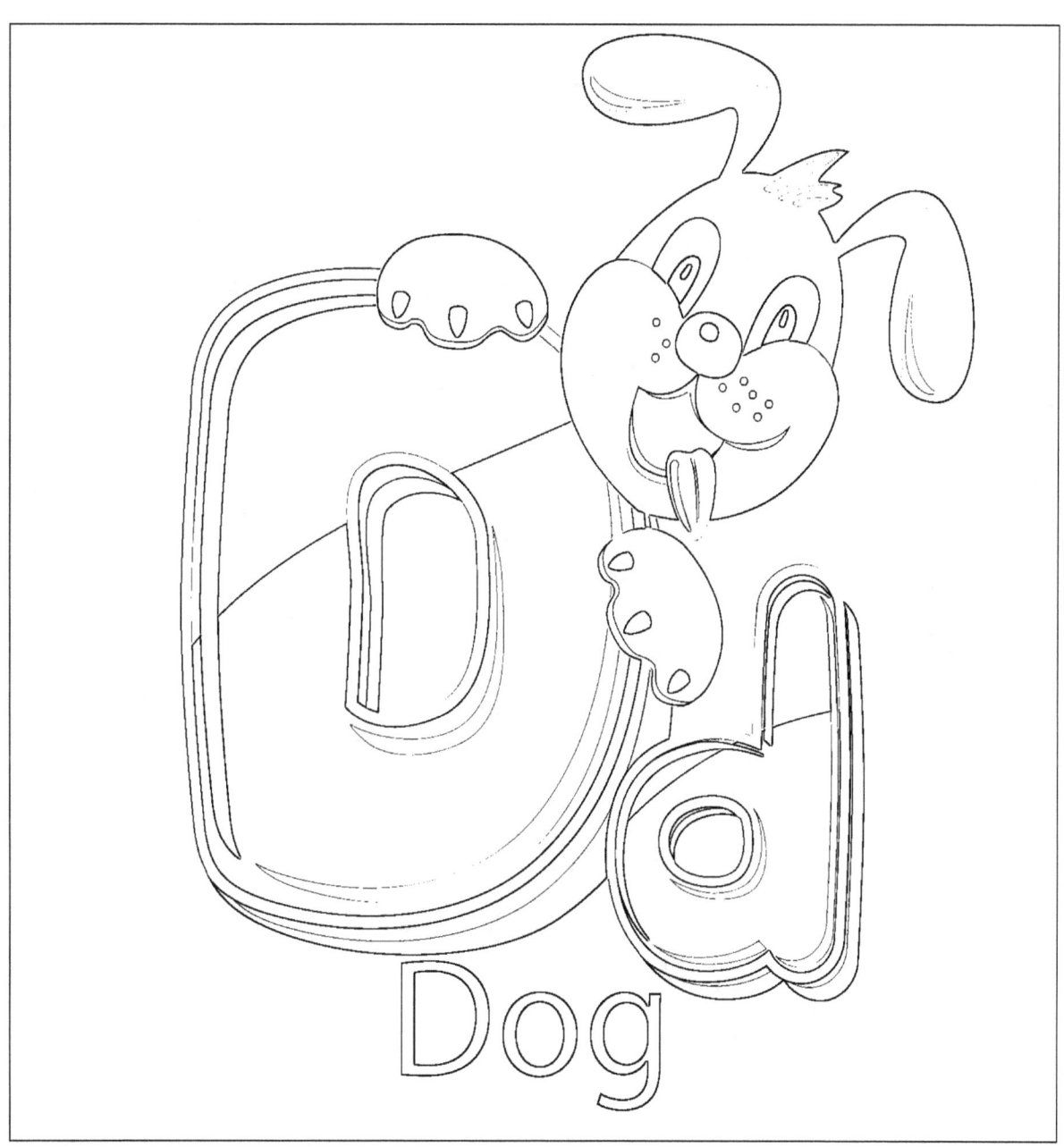

Dog

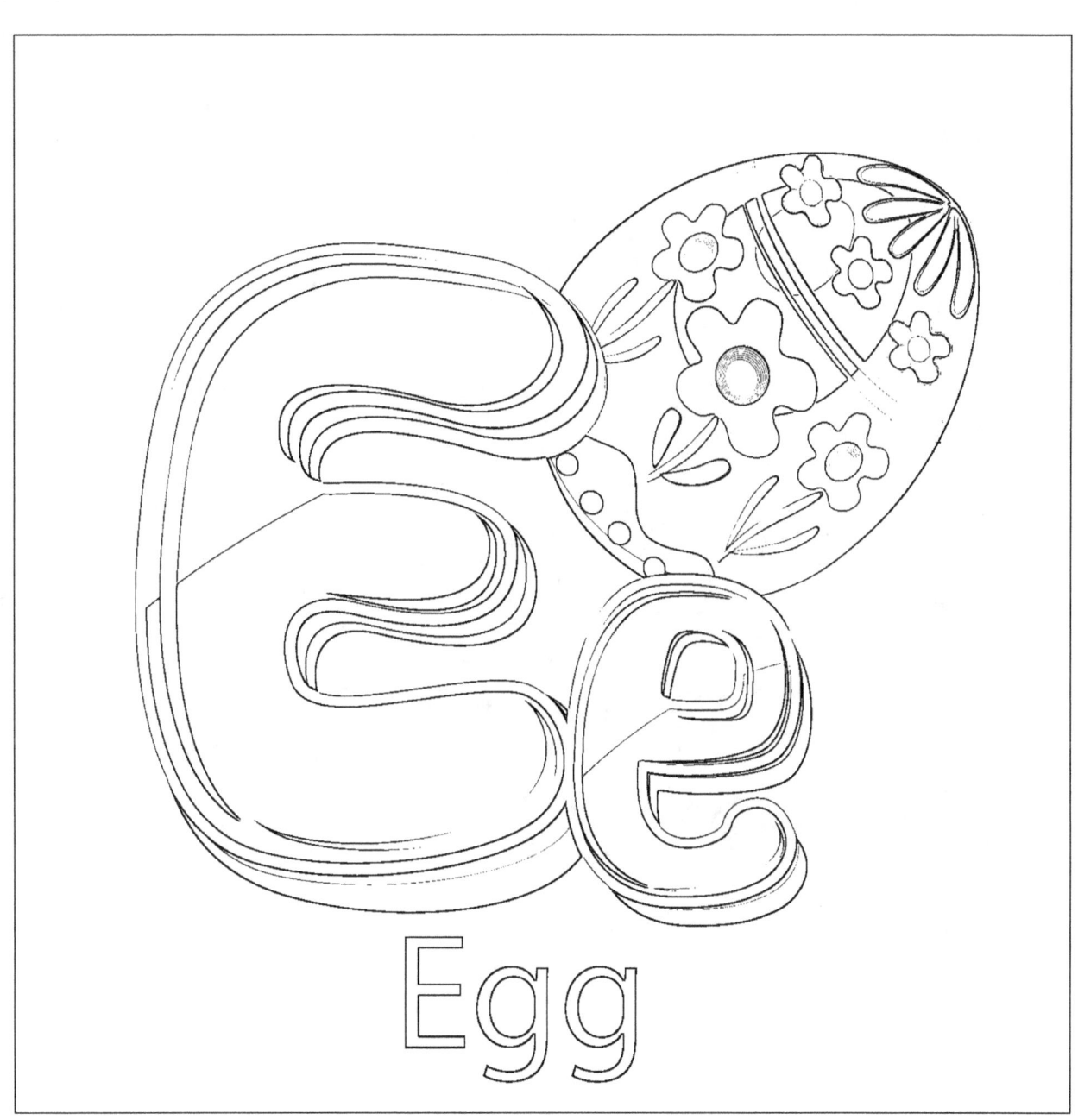

Egg

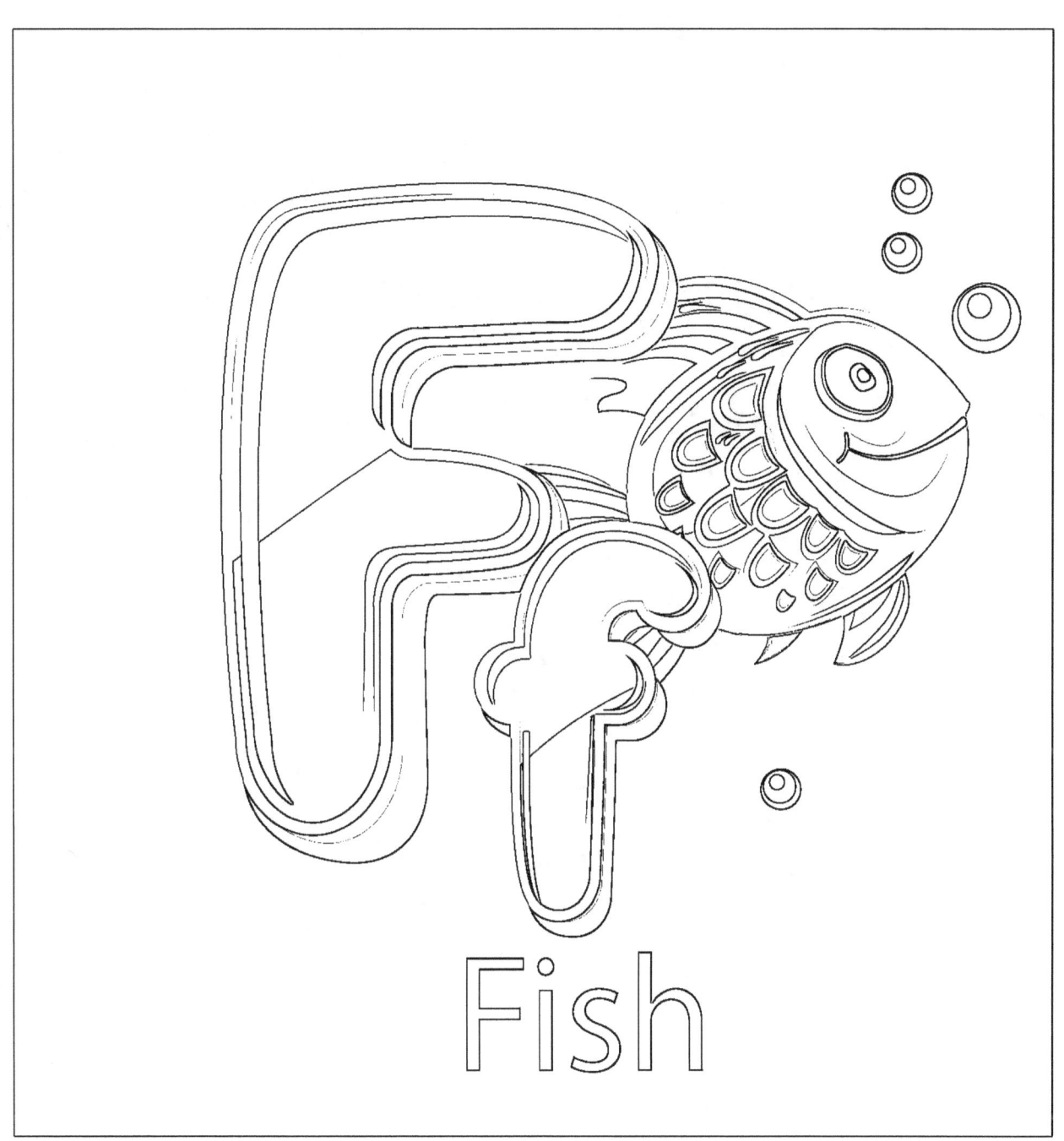

Fish

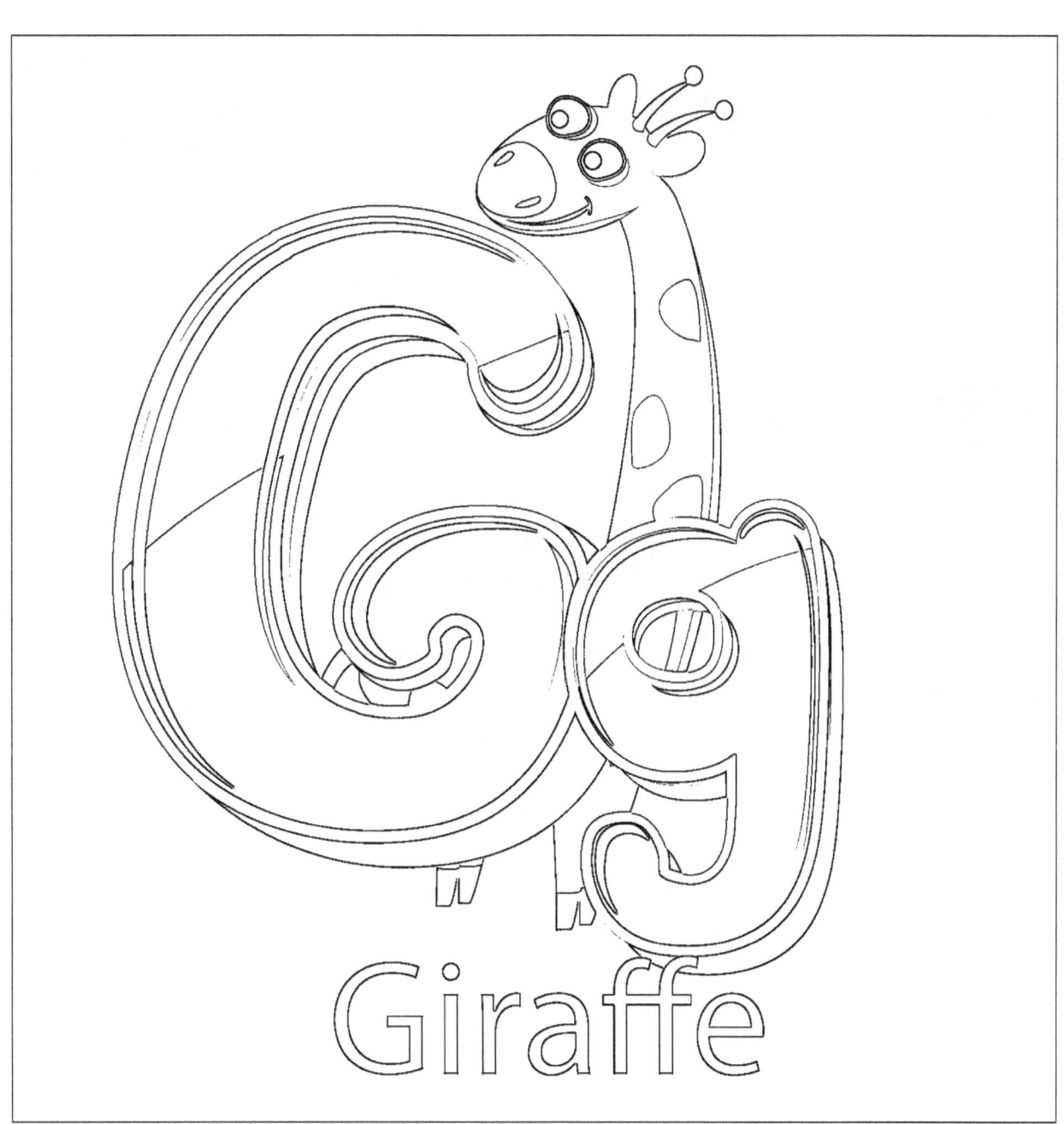

Giraffe

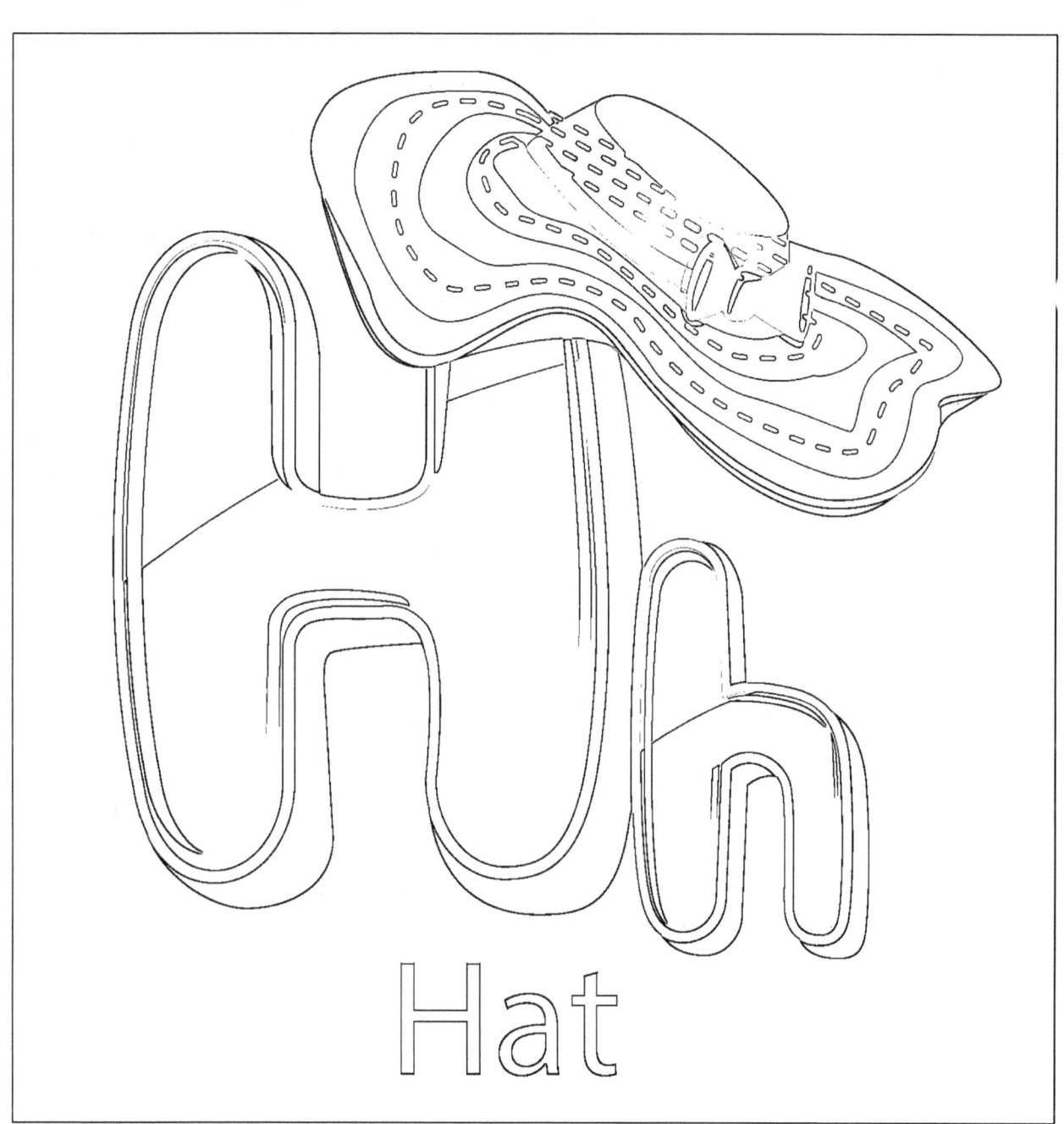

Hat

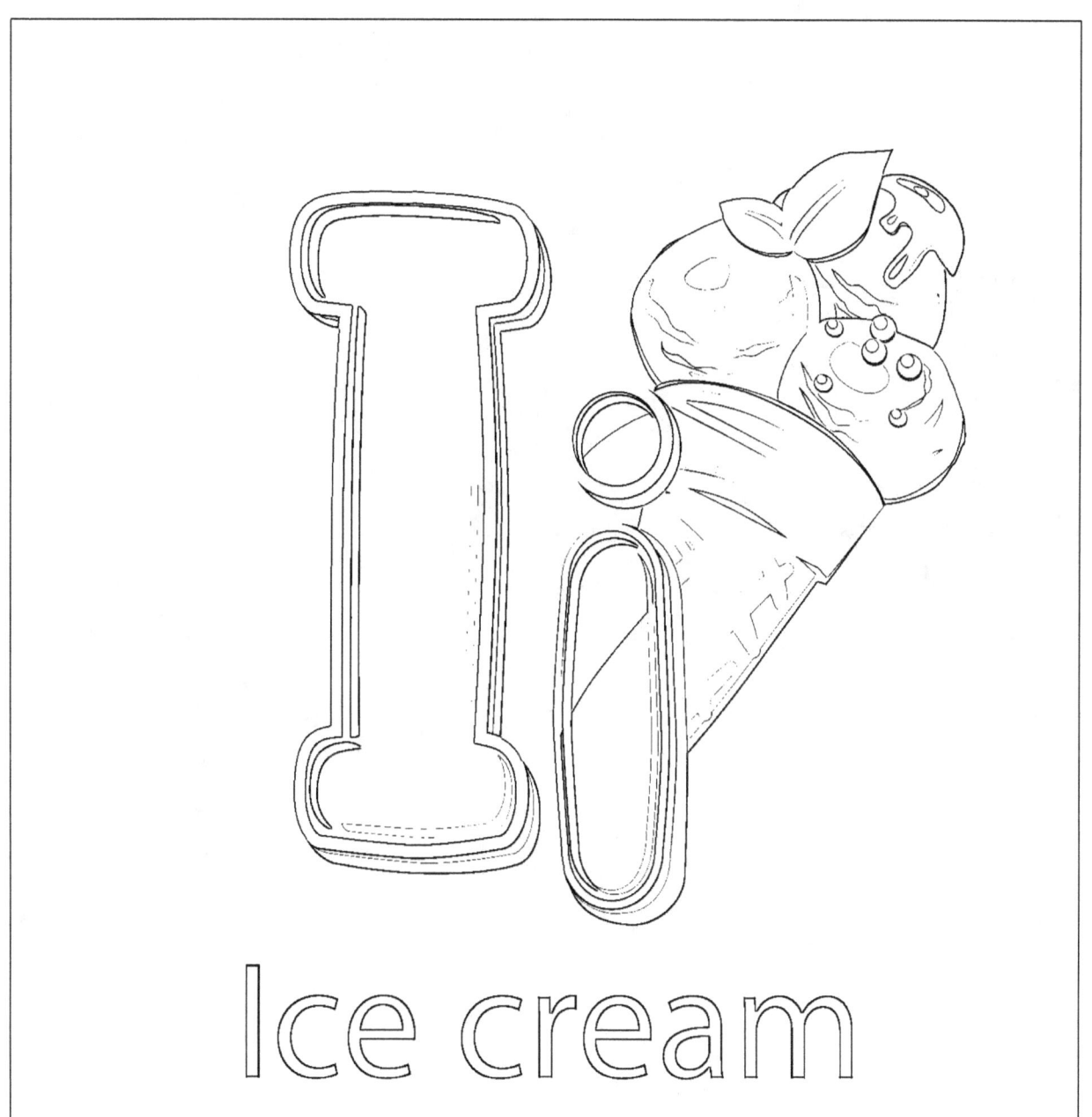

Ice cream

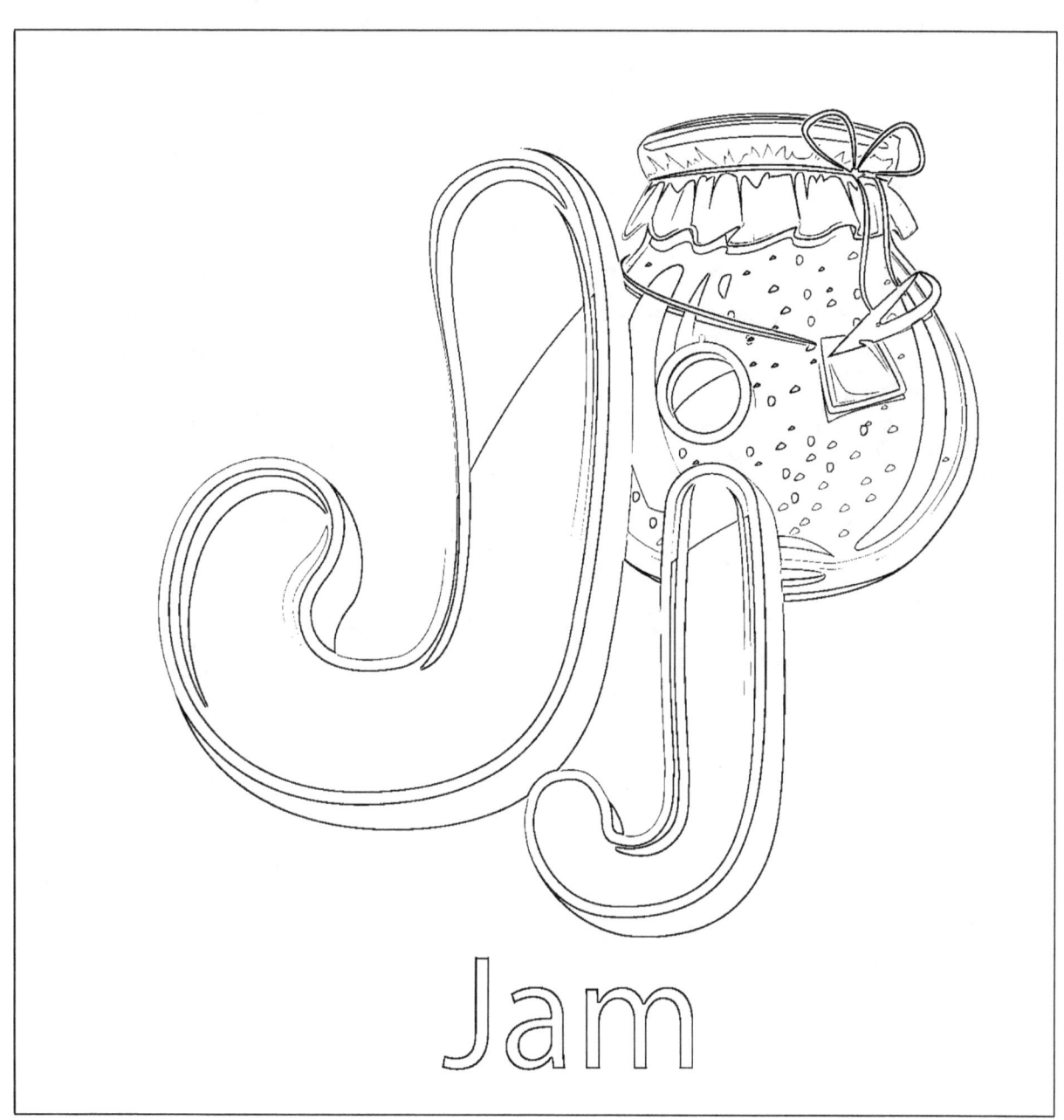

Jam

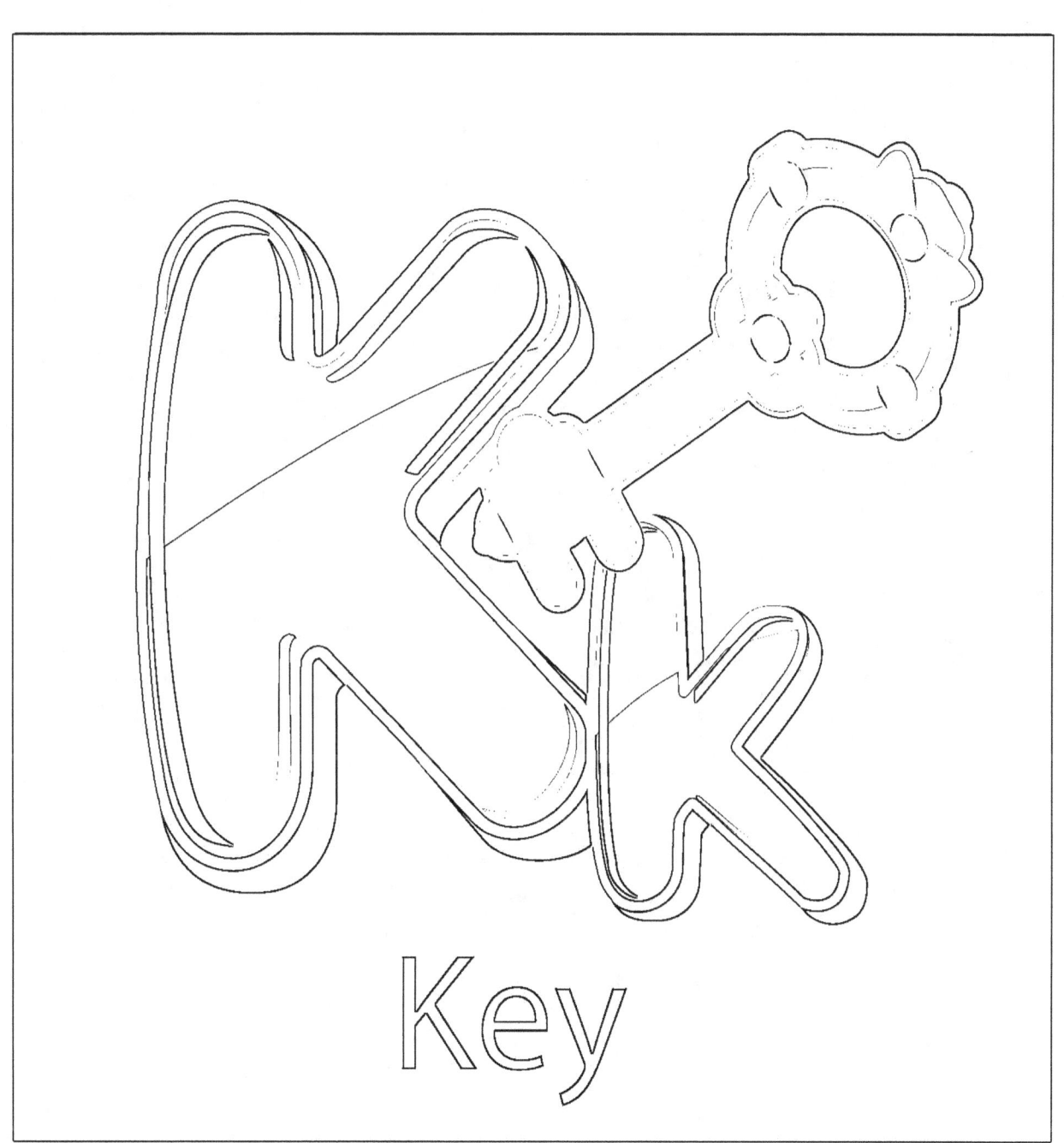

Key

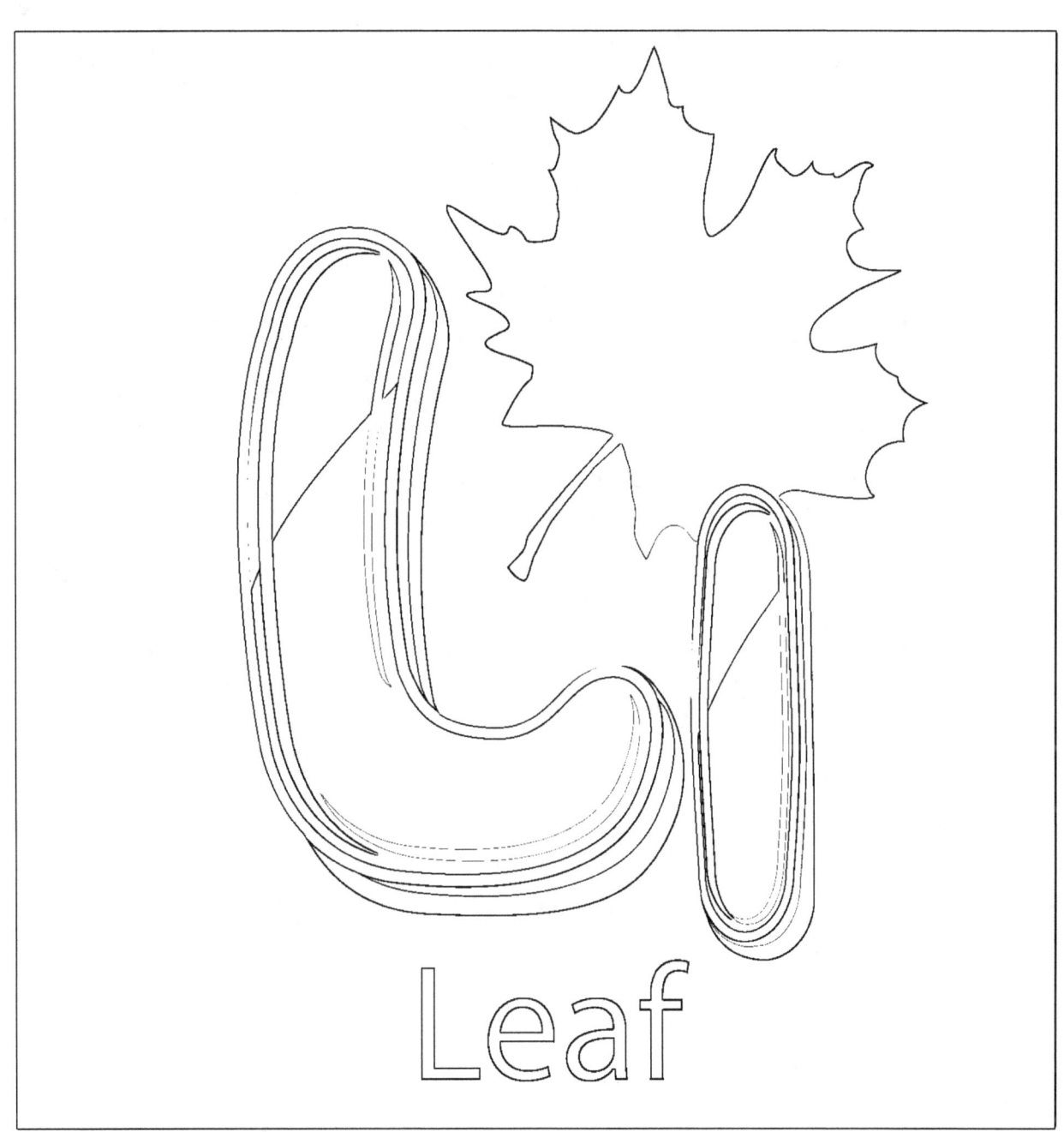

Leaf

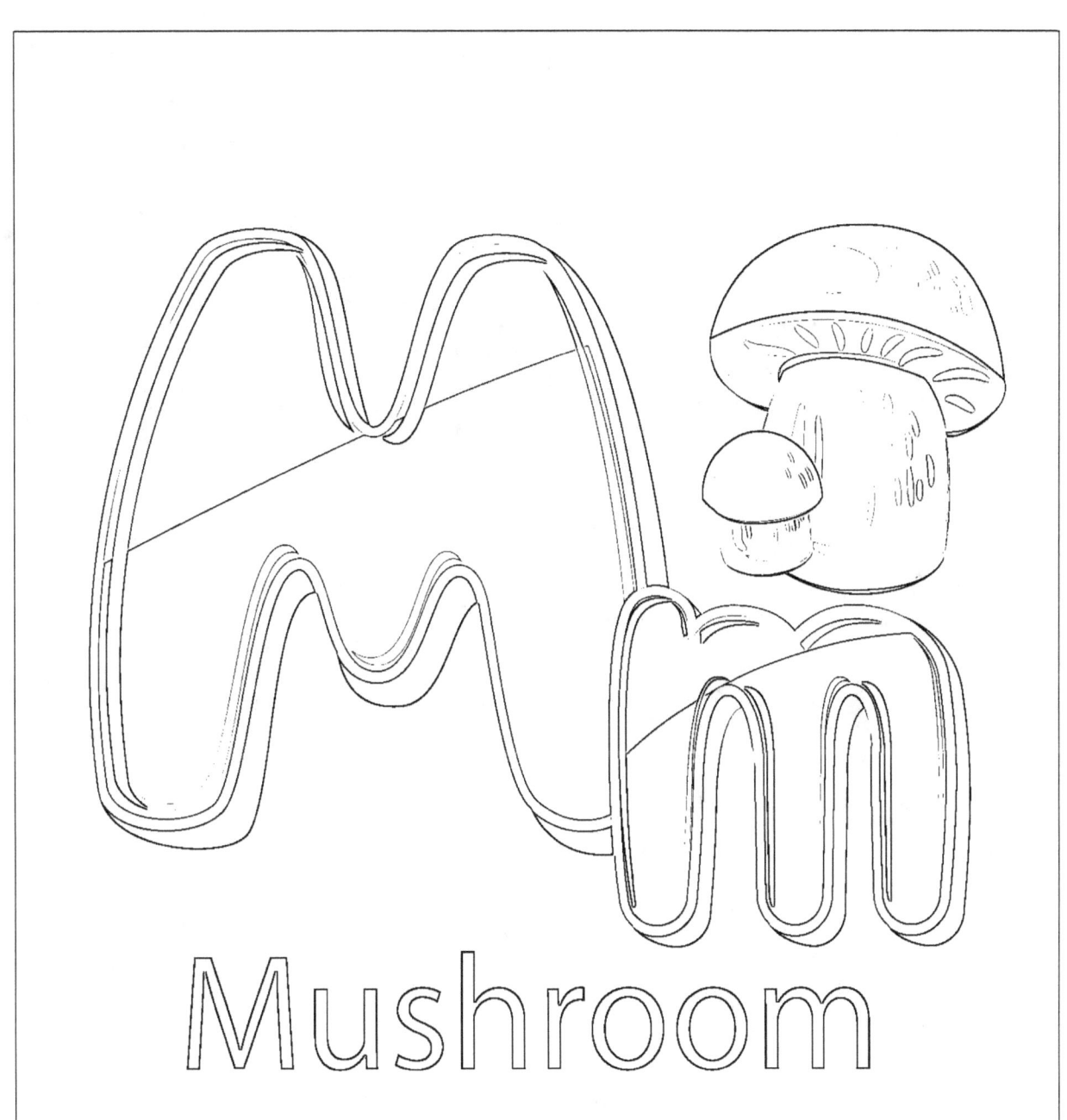

Mushroom

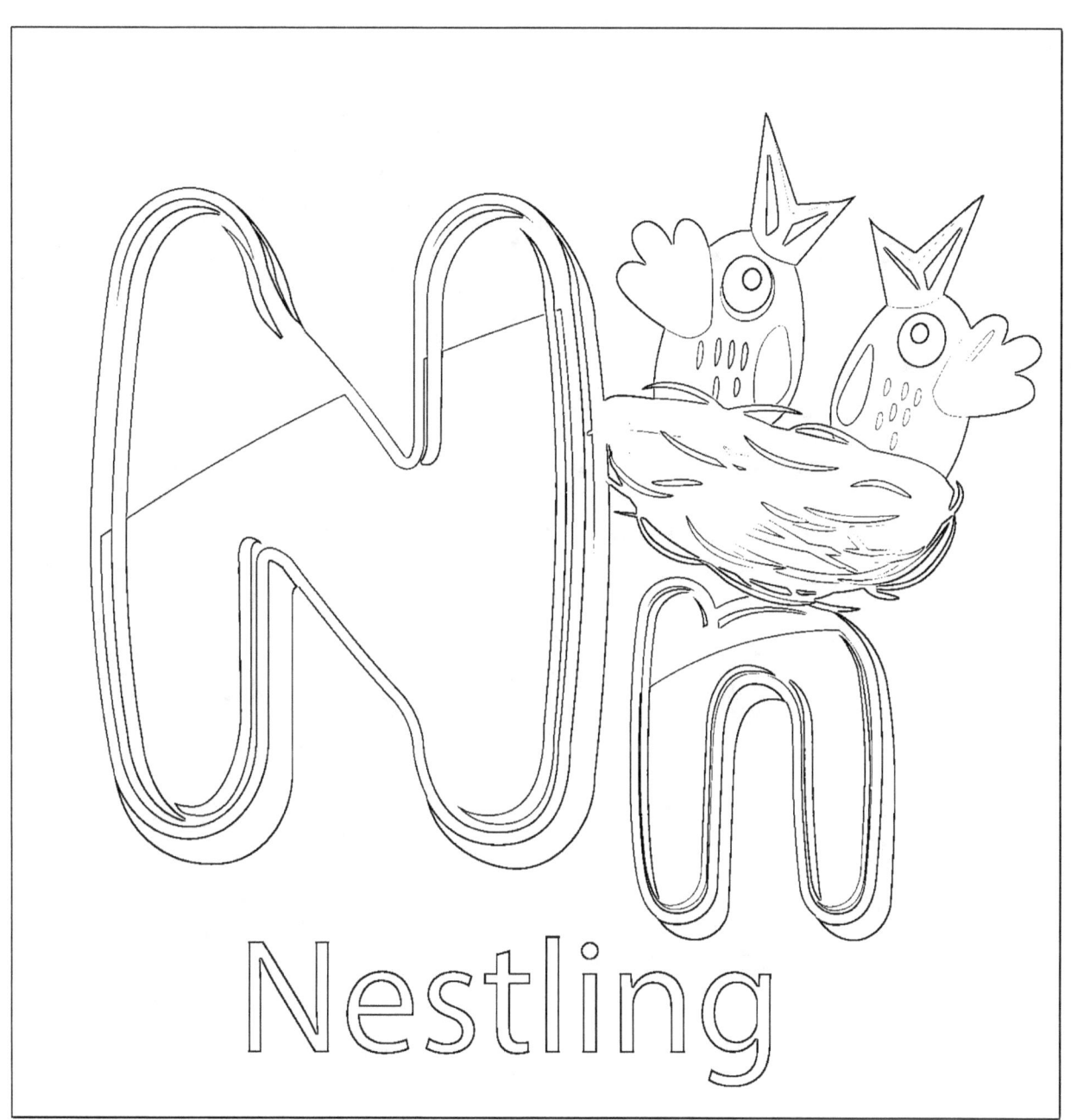

Nestling

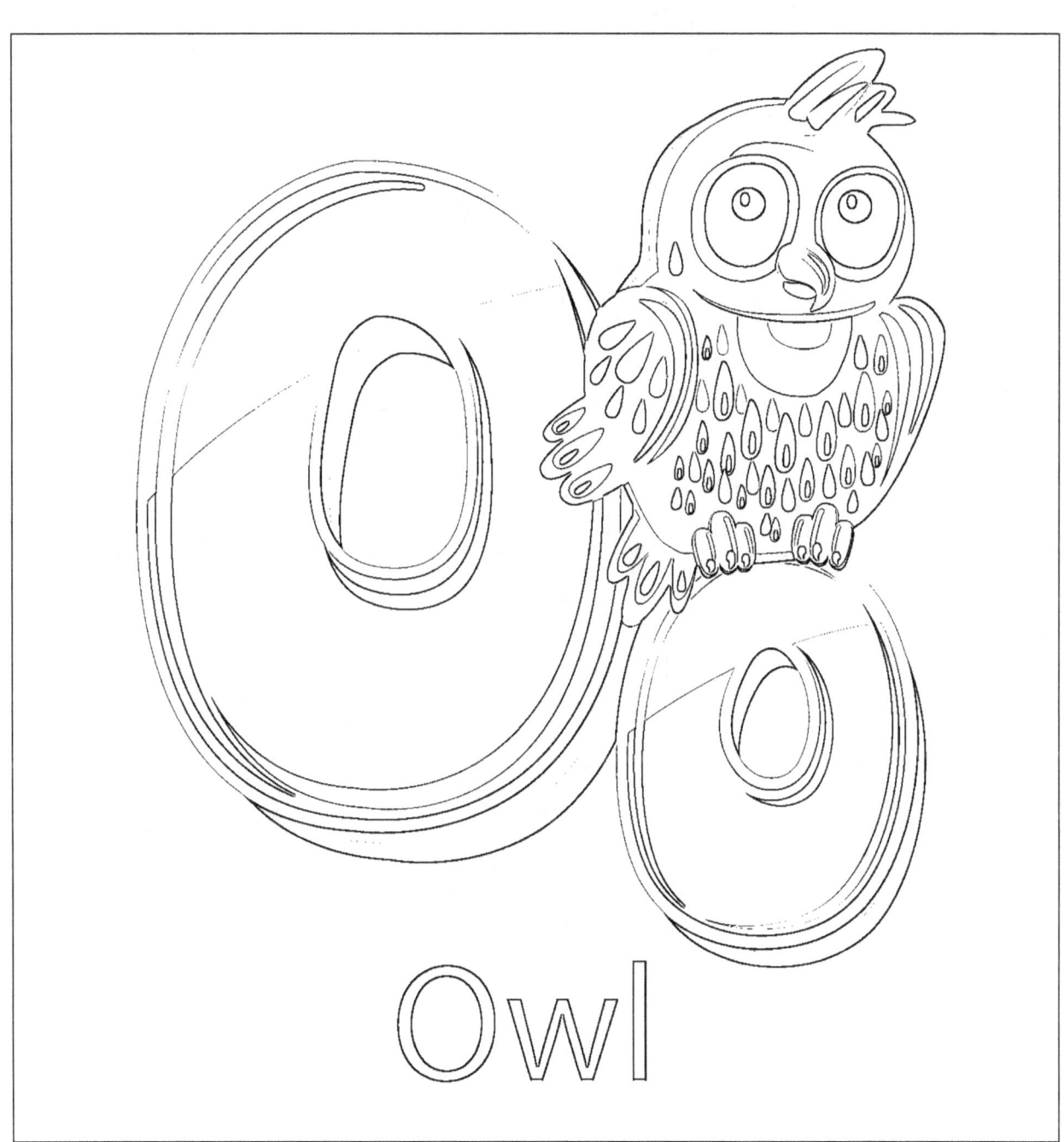

Owl

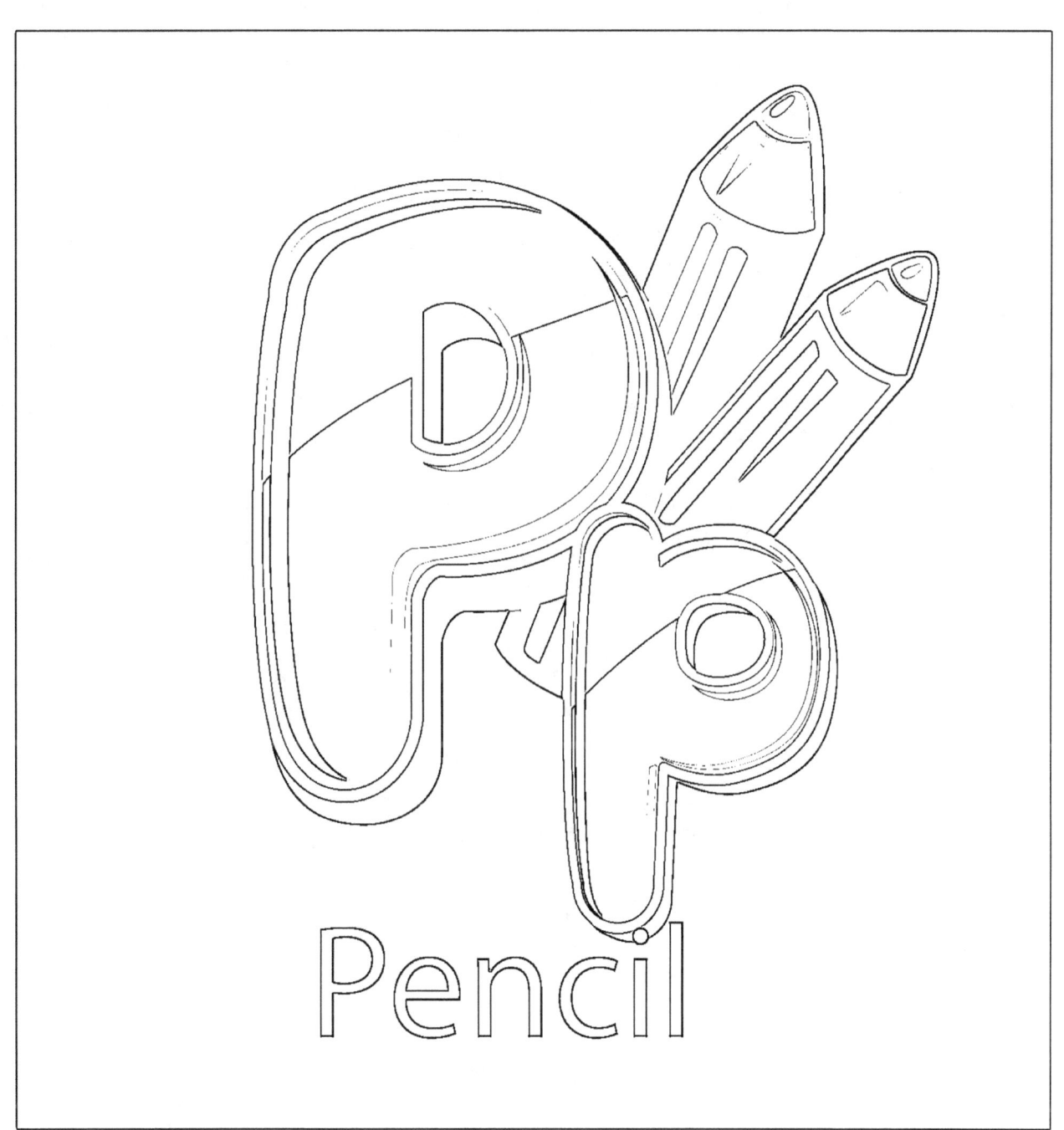

Pencil

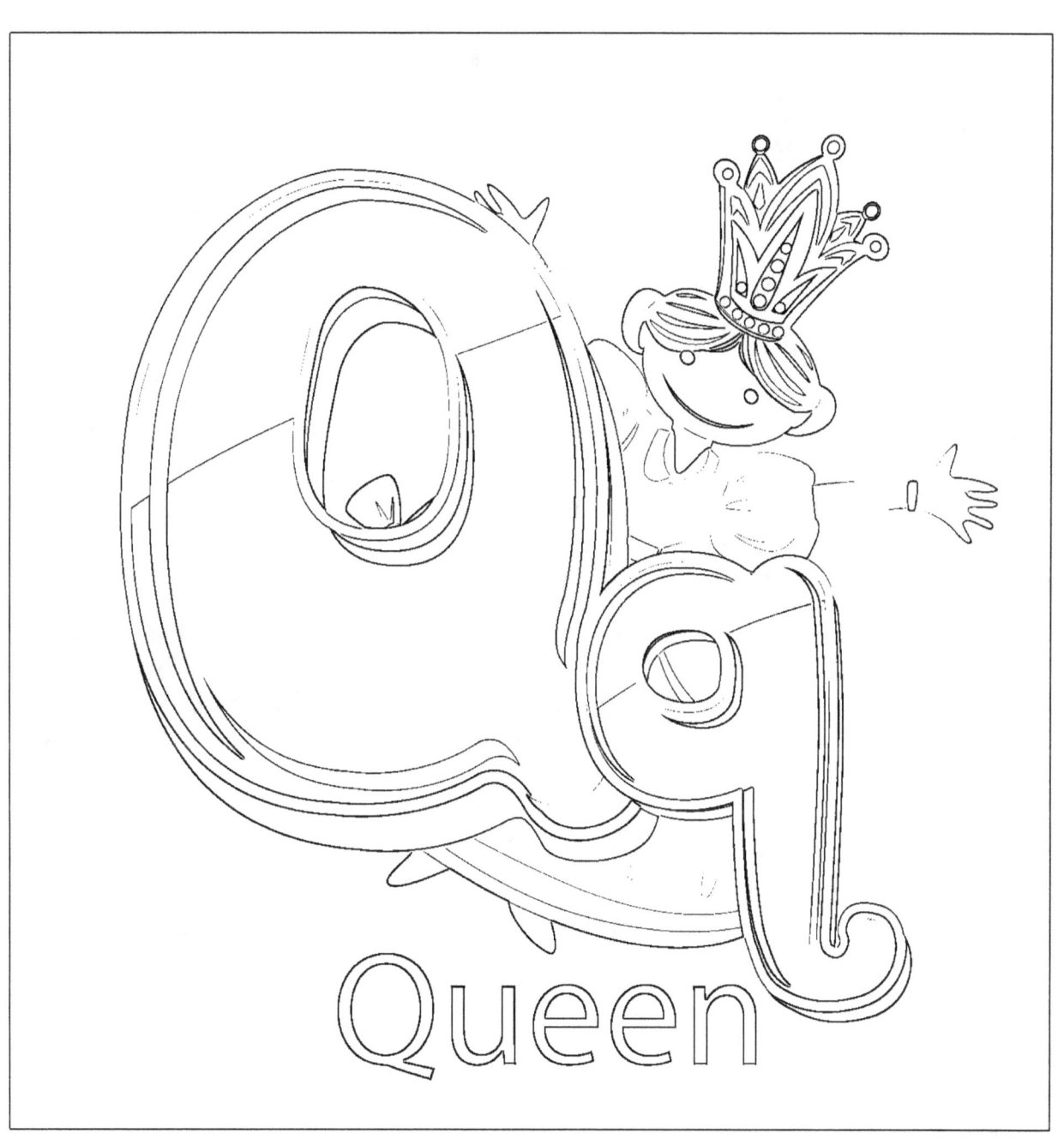

Queen

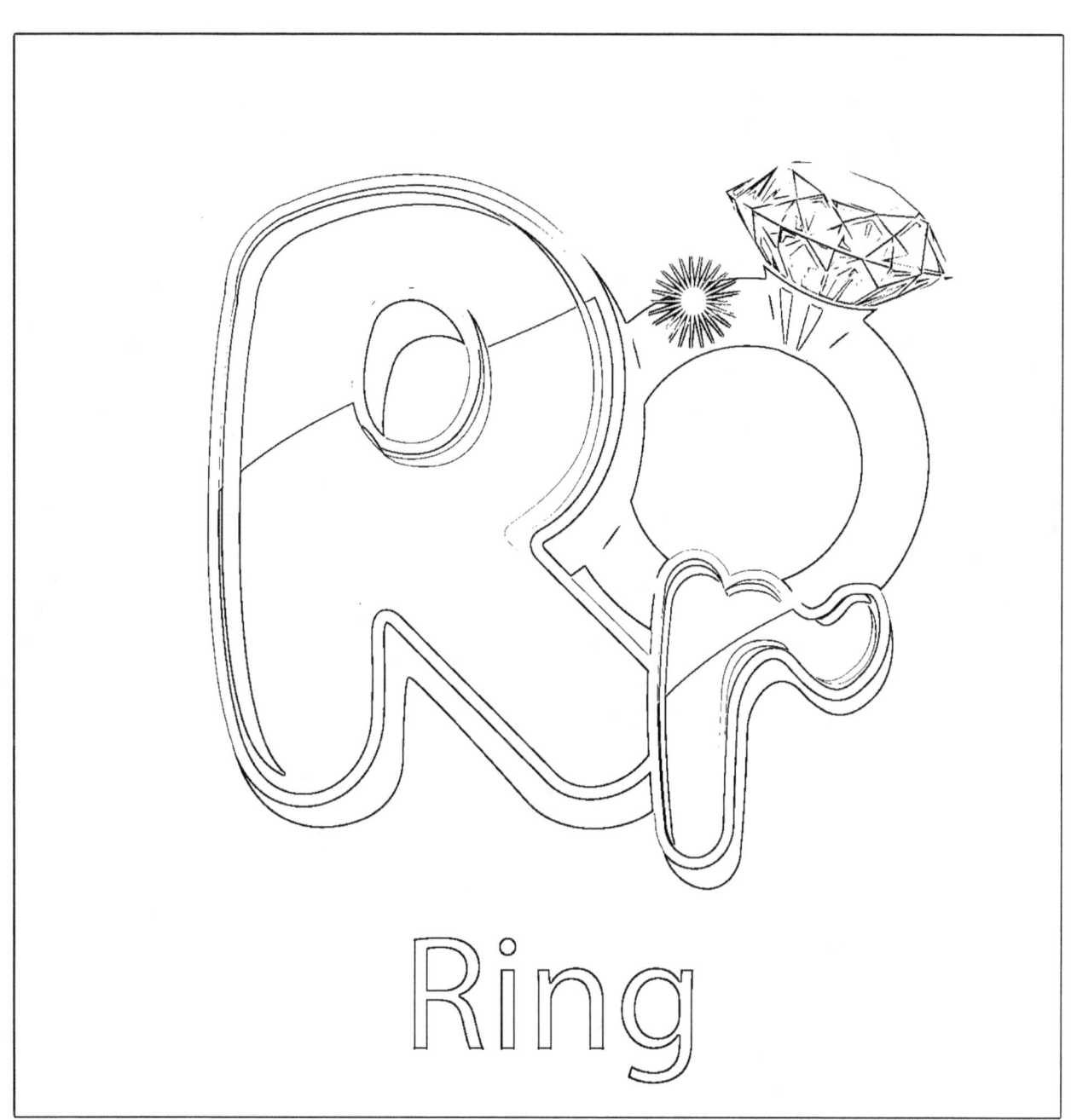

Ring

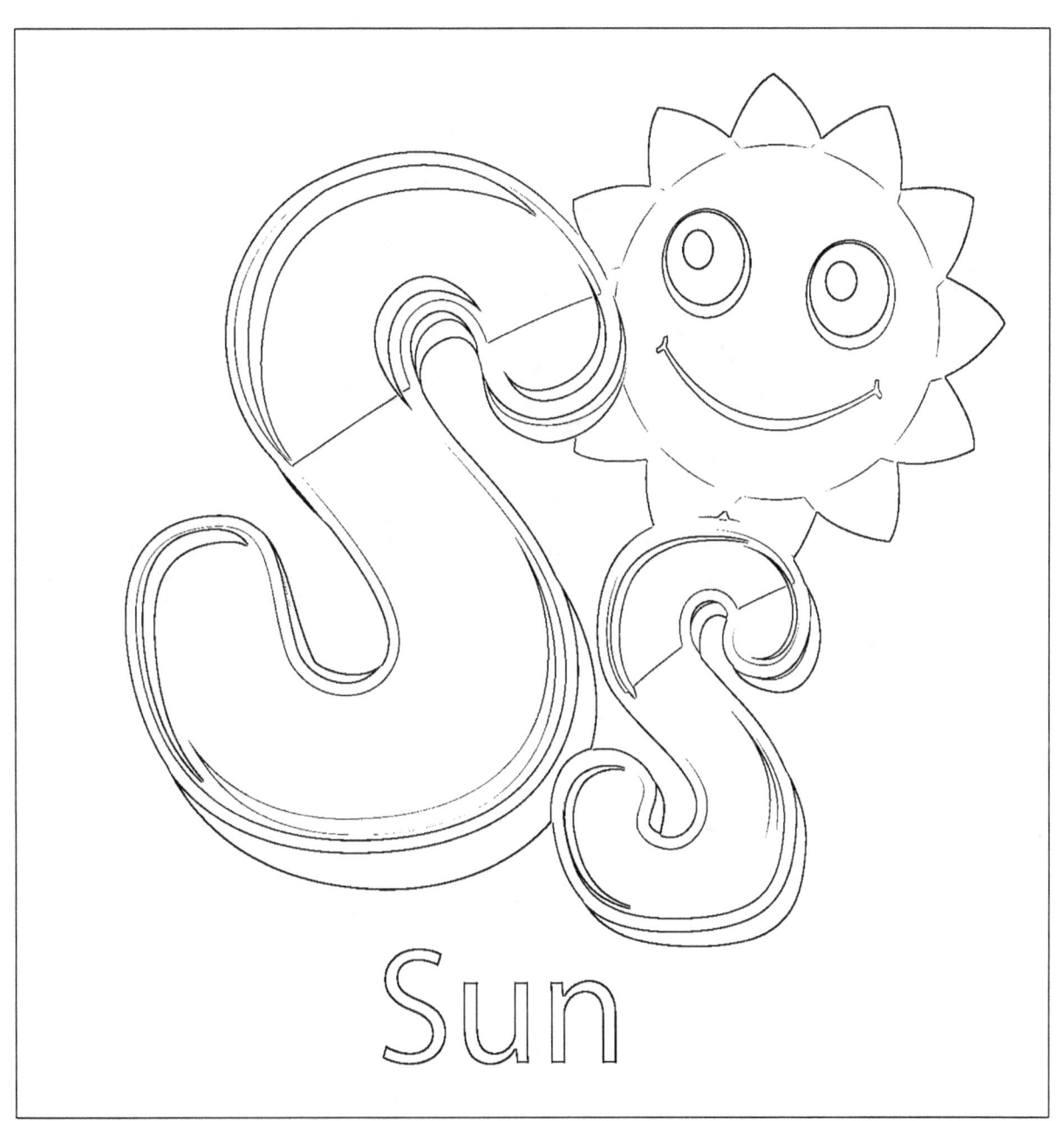

Sun

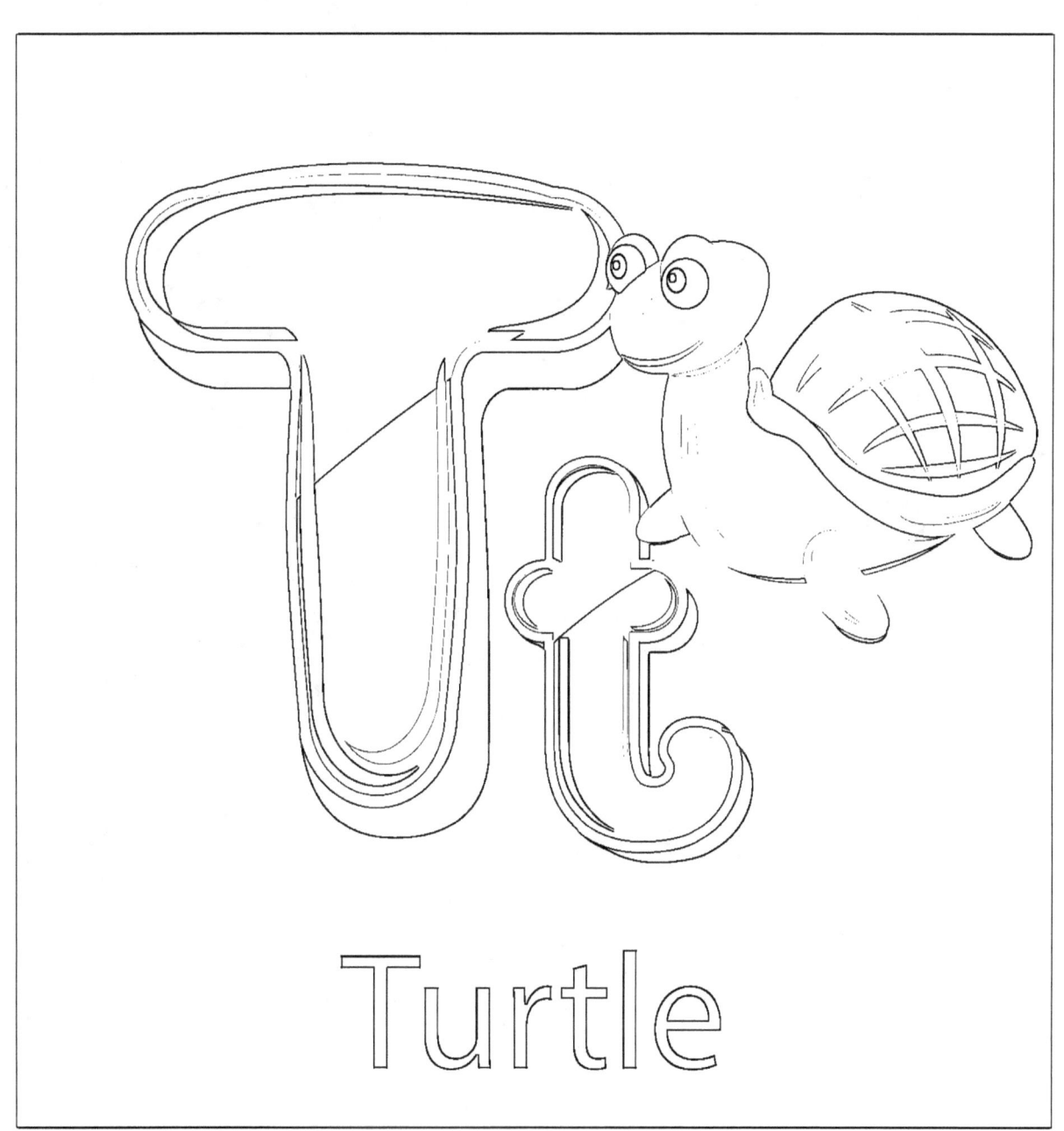

Turtle

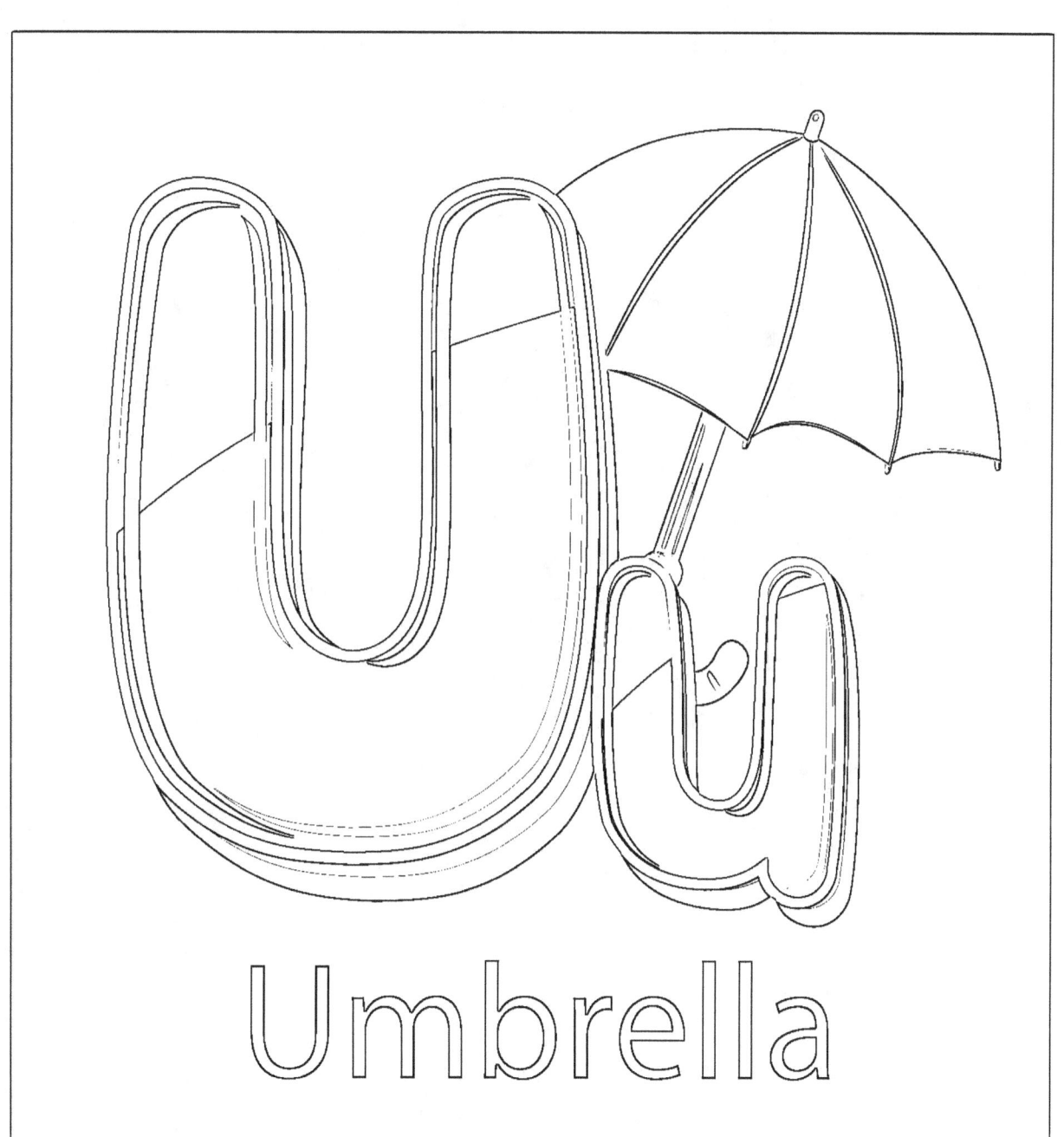

Umbrella

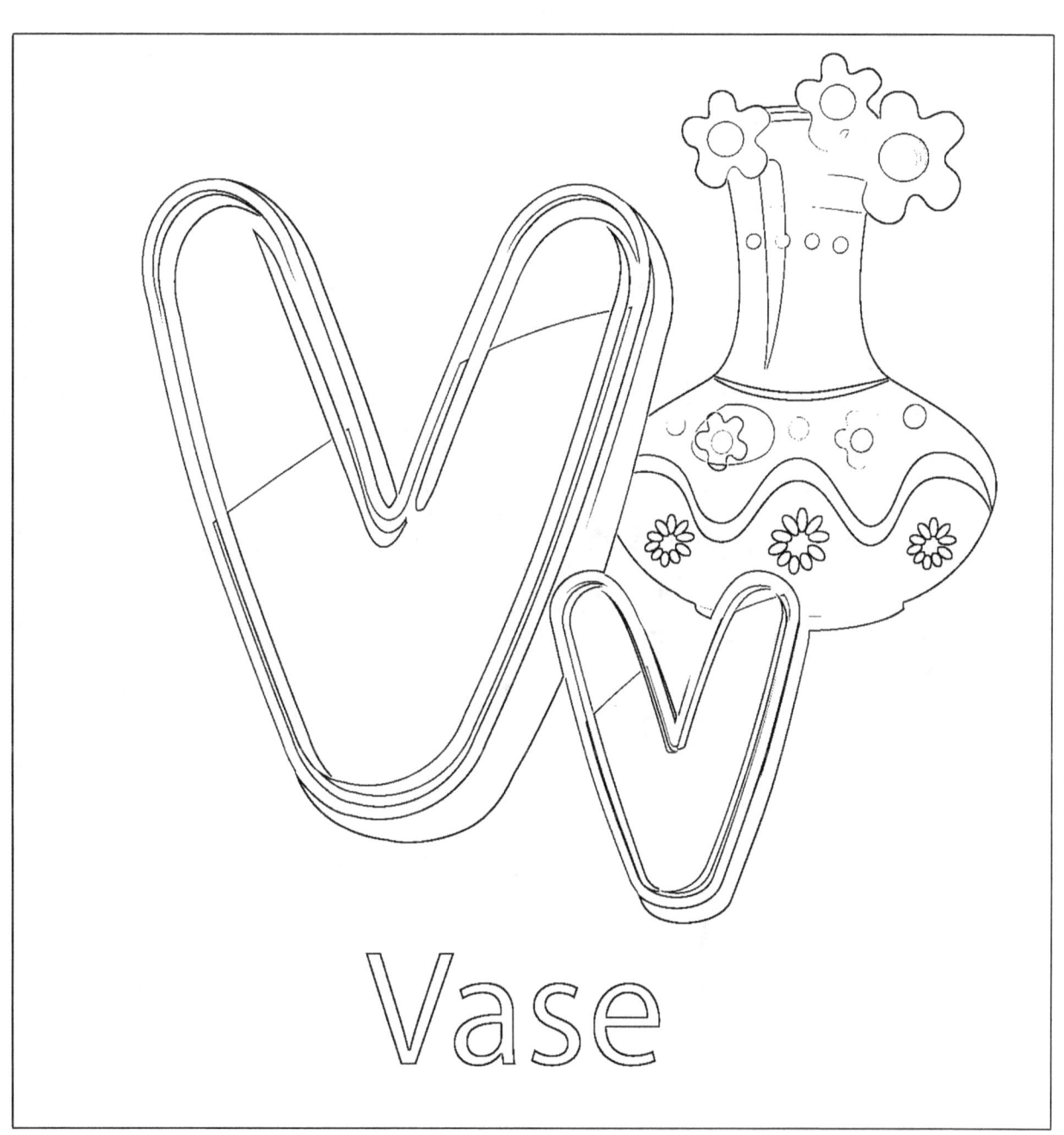

Vase

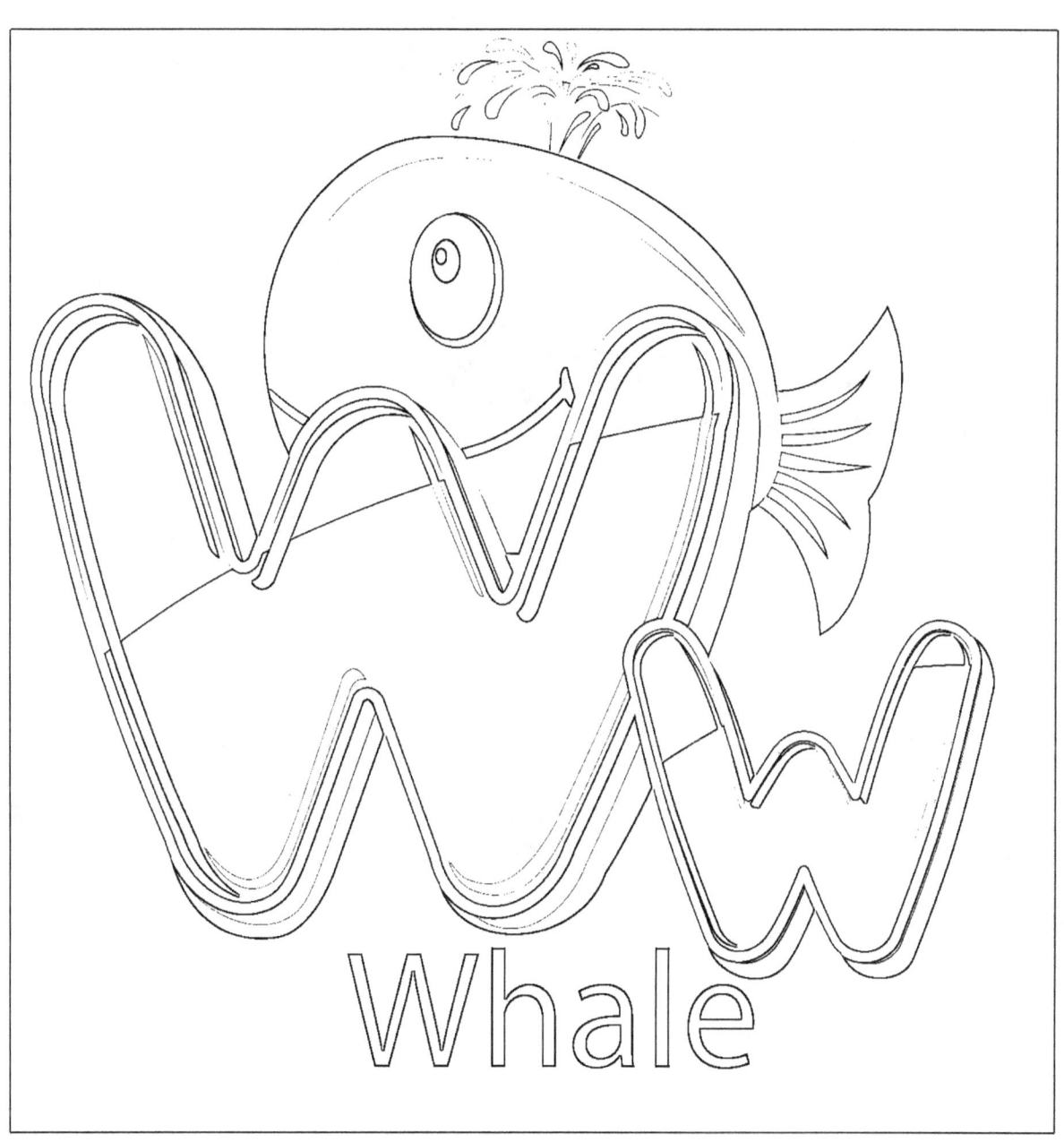

Whale

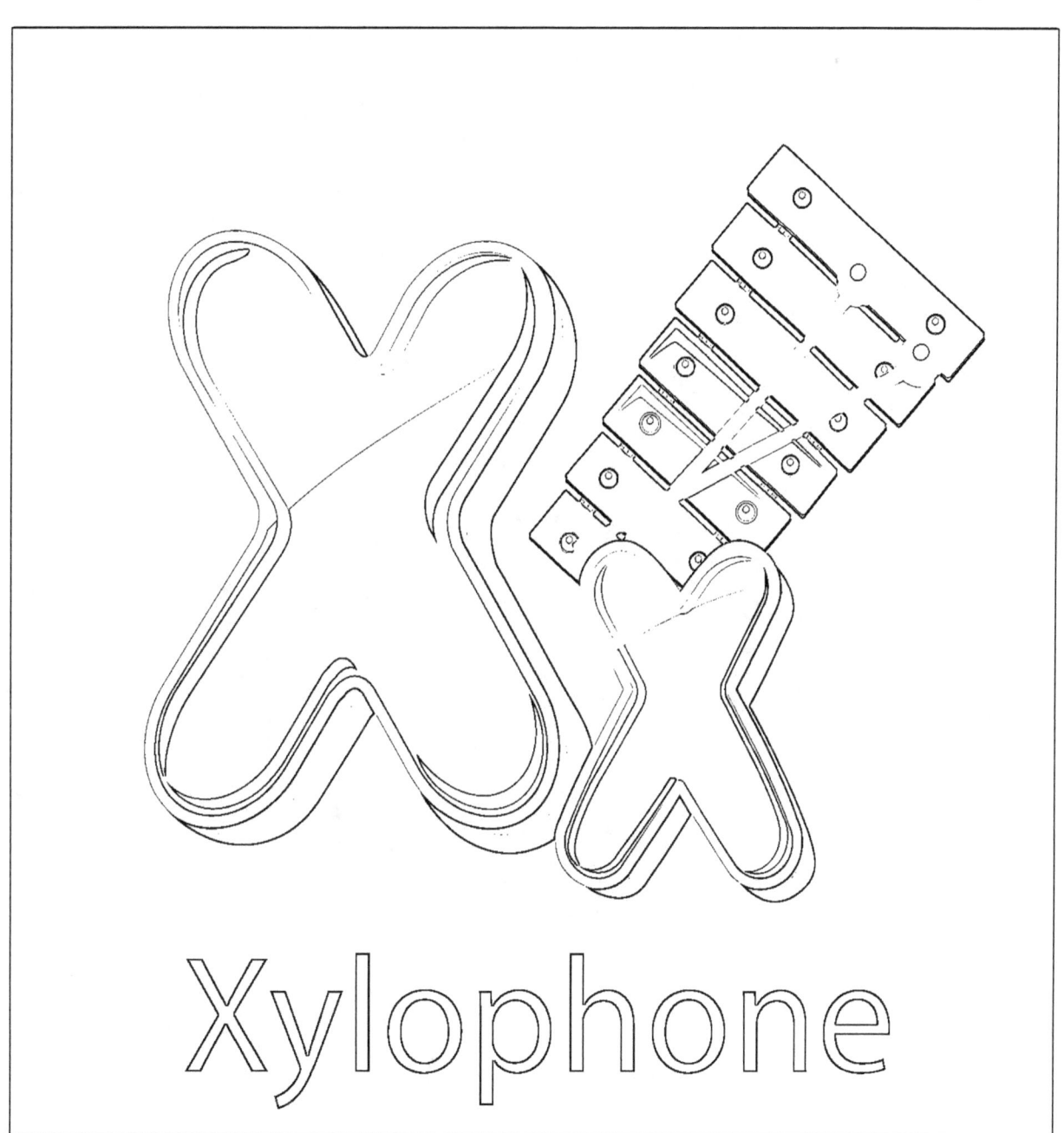

Xylophone

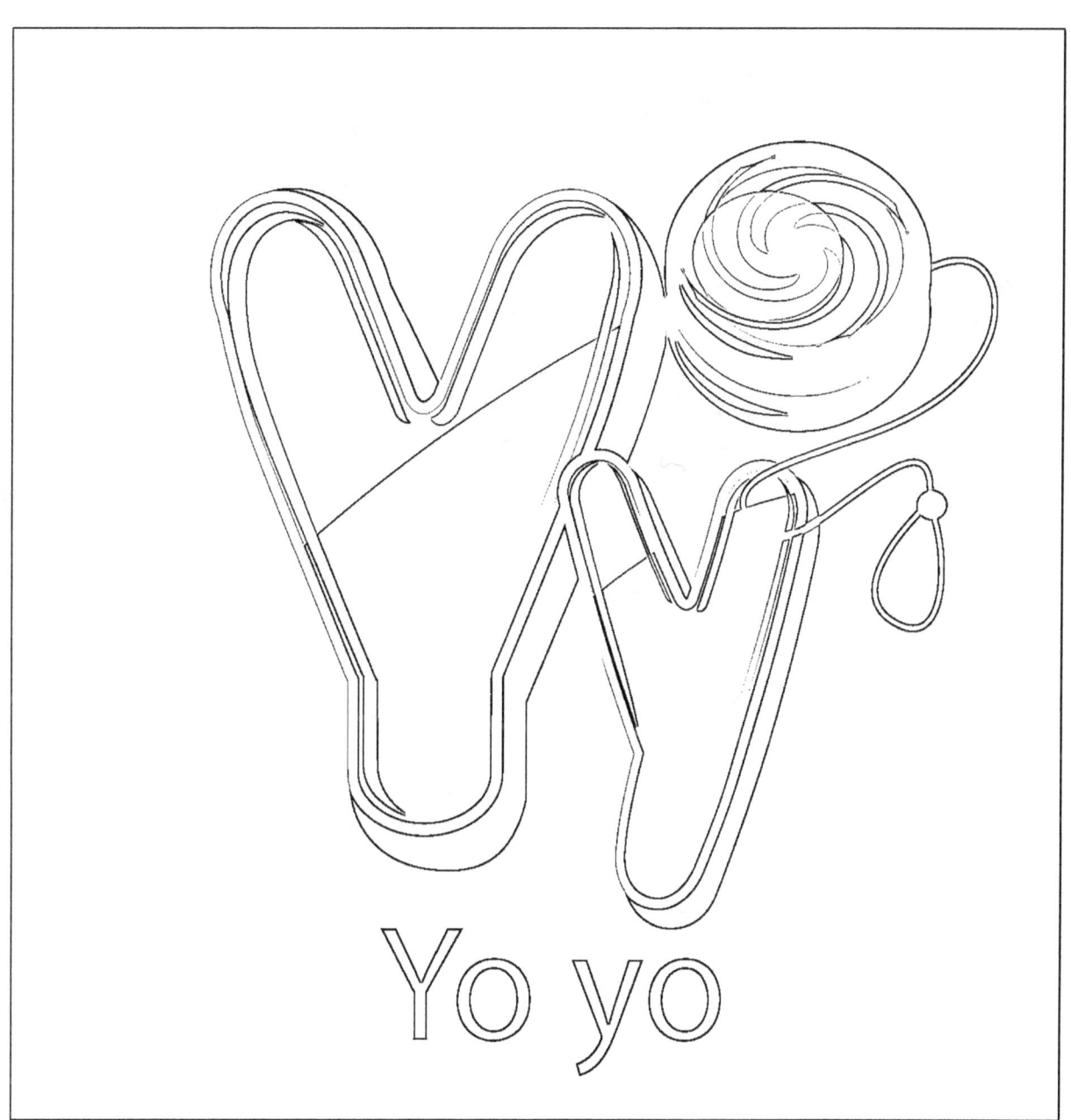

Yo yo

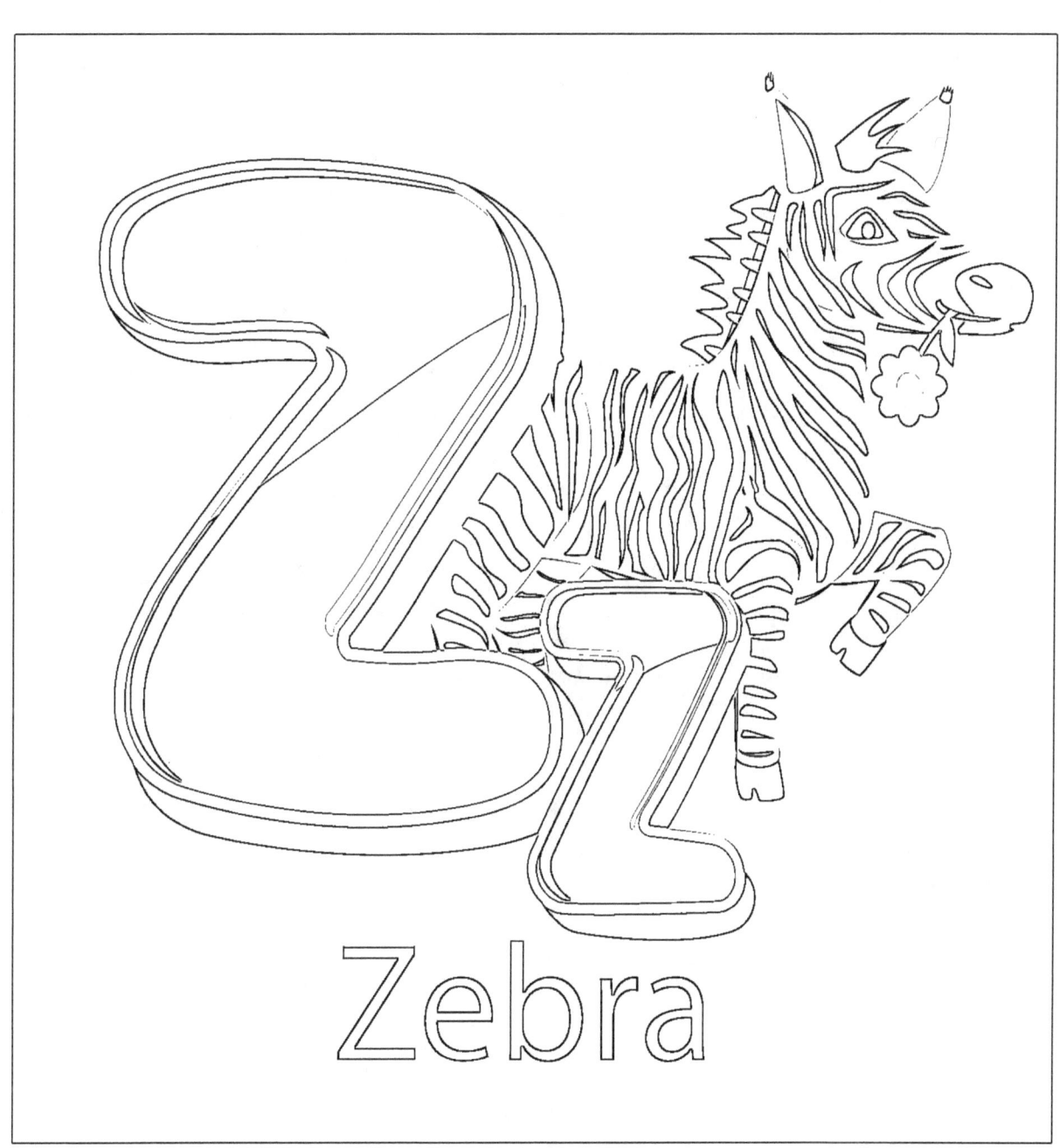

Zebra

www.ingramcontent.com/pod-product-compliance
Lightning Source LLC
Chambersburg PA
CBHW081619170526
45166CB00009B/3032